MANIFESTOS FOR THE 21ST CENTURY

SERIES EDITORS: URSULA OWEN AND JUDITH VIDAL-HALL

Free expression is as high on the agenda as it has ever been, though not always for the happiest of reasons. Here, distinguished writers address the issue of censorship in a complex and fragile world where people with widely different cultural habits and beliefs are living in close proximity, where offence is easily taken, and where words, images and behaviour are coming under the closest scrutiny. These books will surprise, clarify and provoke in equal measure.

Index on Censorship is the only international magazine promoting and protecting free expression. A haven for the censored and silenced, it has built an impressive track record since it was founded 35 years ago, publishing some of the finest writers, sharpest analysts and foremost thinkers in the world. In this series with Seagull Books, the focus will be on questions of rights, liberties, tolerance, silencing, censorship and dissent.

OFFENCE
the jewish case

BRIAN KLUG

LONDON NEW YORK CALCUTTA

Seagull Books 2009

© Brian Klug 2009

ISBN-13   978 1 90649 739 2

British Library Cataloguing-in-Publication Data
A catalogue record for this book is available
from the British Library

Typeset and designed by Seagull Books, Calcutta, India
Printed in Calcutta at Rockwel Offset

For Myke
irreverent and respectful
gentle man, cousin and friend
1949–2009

CONTENTS

2 January 2009, Allentown, Pennsylvania, USA: demonstrators with image of Israeli flag on which the Star of David is replaced by a swastika protest against Israeli invasion of Gaza. Courtesy ADL.

IN THE BEGINNING . . .

In the beginning, before 'Judaism' divides into different kinds and denominations and roams across the face of the earth, is the text: the Hebrew scripture and the story it tells. I use the present tense since the story, in one retelling or another, endures. And I put 'Judaism' in quotes because I am not at all sure that the word fits the thing that it names. Judaism: what is it?

I start with this question because it is fundamental for the remit of this essay. On the one hand, there is nothing that non-Jews can do that is more likely to cause Jews to take offence than misunderstanding or misrepresenting Judaism—if only because Jews generally regard this as *their* prerogative. On the other hand, *giving* offence is virtually a Jewish way of life. This might sound like a throwaway line but it will turn out to be the thought that anchors the whole of the argument. You can call it a claim about Judaism, but it's not: it's a way of *laying* claim to the tradition that goes by that name, which is a rather different matter. But this must keep. First things first.

Aside from this introduction, the essay falls into three parts. In Part One, I examine the standard dictionary definition of Judaism. Calling Judaism a *religion* turns out to be problematic; even calling it *Judaism* can be misleading. The upshot is that the familiar distinction between 'religious' and 'secular' is not adequate to the Jewish case. Some readers, at this point, will object on

the grounds that there is a larger context
that I am ignoring: the resurgence of faith
in the twenty-first century. This, they will
say, poses a threat to the modern world and
gives rise to a 'battle for the Enlightenment'.
Judaism, on this view, comes into the picture
only insofar as it is, precisely, a religion. My
reply, which occupies Part Two of the essay,
offers a critique of 'Enlightenment piety'
and recalls a 'dark side' of Enlightenment
thought: the dominant perception of Judaism
and Jews. Having cleared the ground, in
Part Three, I bring the argument of the
essay to bear on the Jewish case today. I
home-in on the debate over Israel, since
this is the arena that is most conspicuous.
With the earlier discussion of identity in
mind, I explore the complex sensibility that
leads many Jews to create 'no go' areas of
debate. But Judaism in its depths cries out
for outspokenness; or such is the tradition
to which I lay claim at the end. There is a

battle among Jews over the limits of free speech about Israel: this is the context I see for the essay. Call it a battle for Judaism.

Focusing on the Jewish case, I shall inevitably be occupied with those features that single it out. This seems to imply that the Jewish case is exceptional. But I hazard a guess that each of the other cases—Islamic, Sikh, Hindu, Christian and so on—is exceptional too, each in its own way. Each has its own peculiarities that complicate the debate over free speech. Take, for example, the anger provoked in 2006 by the Danish cartoons that caricatured Prophet Mohammed, including one where he is wearing a turban in the shape of a bomb with a lit fuse: I am certain that this was about more than the breaking of a religious taboo (Klug 2006: 47). However, such controversies and their complications are outside the scope of this essay. I shall not comment on them except indirectly. The discussion of the Enlightenment is broader; it includes a critical assessment of one approach to the defence of free speech, an approach that is prominent in contemporary 'progressive' circles. But I do not explore the ramifications for other identities. My subject is not offence in general, but specifically the Jewish case.

WHAT IS JUDAISM?

According to my *Cassell's New English Dictionary* (nineteenth edition, July 1960), given to me as a barmitzvah present by Mr and Mrs Shindler (says the note I wrote on the inside front cover, probably using one of the Parker 61 fountain pens I also received as a gift, the giving of fountain pens as barmitzvah presents being part of the unwritten law), 'Judaism' means: 'The religious doctrines and rites of the Jews, according to the law of Moses'. Similarly, the latest edition of the *Concise Oxford English Dictionary* defines

it as 'the monotheistic religion of the Jews,
based on the Old Testament and the Talmud'. This is the standard line: Judaism is a
religion, a religion of a particular sort.

But is it? I hesitate to call it so, given
the connotations of the word (to which I
shall return). And the polysyllabic
'monotheistic' strikes me as rather stilted,
rather Greek; as though Judaism were an
Oxford philosophical society for the ad-
vancement of the thesis that the sum total
of divine beings is less than two and more
than zero. I'm not even sure about calling
Judaism *Judaism*: the 'ism' ending could
imply a system of belief or set of principles.
But while something of the sort can certainly
be found in connection with 'Judaism'—some
of my best Jewish friends are believers—it's
not the thing itself.

Then what is this thing called 'Judaism'?
And who gave it its name? The name is not
in the Hebrew scripture; nor could it be, for

there is no word in classical Hebrew that corresponds to the English word 'Judaism'; nor is there a word for 'religion'. Suppose Moses was to descend from the clouds today, holding yet another copy of the Ten Commandments aloft: 'Welcome back, Moses,' we say, 'O founder of the *religion* of *Judaism*.' He would not have the foggiest idea what we were on about.[1] Judging by his track record at Sinai, he would likely take offence and dash the tablets of stone to the ground, declaring despairingly, 'They just don't get it.'

Calling Judaism a Religion

We shall get back to the word 'Judaism' shortly. As regards the term 'religion', Louis Jacobs explains: 'As an abstract term the word "religion"' is found in neither the Bible nor the Talmud, both of which use concrete language.' He adds:

It was not until the Middle Ages, when Christianity and Islam had emerged, that Jewish theologians were obliged to consider Judaism as a religion, different from these two religions but resembling them in certain respects. For purposes of discussion and debate a term for religion had to be coined. The term the medieval thinkers used, *dat*, derived from a Persian word found in late passages in the Bible, originally meant law, in the very concrete sense of a particular way of conduct, but now came to denote religion in the abstract (1995: 418).

In other words, Jewish thinkers adapted their way of talking about Judaism for the sake of having a common framework with their non-Jewish contemporaries. But the larger culture, in Europe, was predominantly Christian. As Norman Solomon sees it, this means that talk about Judaism is inherently loaded. In the introduction to his *Historical Dictionary of Judaism*, he calls this 'the framework problem':

> Judaism cannot be presented in vacuo.
> The reader who inhabits a Christian en-
> vironment—and essentially that includes
> everyone who reads English, for the
> English language is in part an artefact of
> Christian civilization—inevitably comes
> to Judaism with a cargo of Christian con-
> cepts and assumptions (1998: 1).

It is partly on account of this problem
that I hesitate to call Judaism a 'religion'.
For, even to the extent that it makes sense
to apply the word to Judaism, it does not
necessarily make the *same* sense that it
makes when it is applied to Christianity: the
one 'religion' is organized around the notion of peoplehood, the other around the
concept of a church. A similar complication
arises with calling Judaism a 'faith'.

With words like these, the 'cargo' lies
concealed inside language that is shared by
both traditions—and by others. But it can
also reside in words that, without the reader
knowing it, are not part of the vocabulary of

Judaism. Take, for example, the term 'the
Old Testament'. It is how people in general
refer to the Hebrew scripture, but it is not a
neutral term. It is certainly not a *Jewish*
name for the text. The Jewish name is
'Tanakh', a Hebrew acronym for the three
bodies of literature that make up the canon.
From a Jewish point of view, the text is, yes,
old, even ancient; but it is not an earlier
model of a new and improved product; not
'the Old' as distinct from 'the New'. The
name reflects a *Christian* point of view on
the scripture and tends to stir up a swarm
of associations in the mind of the reader:
vague notions imbibed with mother's milk
about 'the God the Jews worship'. You don't
have to be Christian to join the mental
dots. Nor is it a matter of official doctrine;
the picture of Judaism that emerges when
the dots are joined isn't sanctioned by the
Church today, if it ever was. The 'cargo' is
in the culture. It is in the air we breathe;

and being an atheist does not make you impervious.

A case in point is the passage that opens 'The God Hypothesis', in *The God Delusion* by dyed-in-the-wool unbeliever Richard Dawkins:

> The God of the Old Testament is arguably the most unpleasant character in all fiction: jealous and proud of it; a petty, unjust, unforgiving control-freak; a vindictive, bloodthirsty ethnic cleanser; a misogynistic, homophobic, racist, infanticidal, genocidal, filicidal, pestilential, megalomaniacal, sadomasochistic, capriciously malevolent bully (2006: 31).

Dawkins, whether he is aware of it or not, invokes a stock figure. Though he does take it a mite further than usual, it's basically the same hoary cliché from an old, familiar script, trite and untrue, that inscribes the difference between Christianity and Judaism as the chasm that separates mercifulness from

vengeance, gentleness from cruelty, uncon-
ditional love from pedantic legalism; in
short, New Testament from Old. Not that
Dawkins is in the business of batting for one
religion against another; he is derisory
about the 'insipidly opposite Christian face,
"Gentle Jesus meek and mild" '. It is the
fact that he sees these two faces as oppo-
sites, plus the opposite features that he
sees, which makes this passage a case in
point.

Be that as it may, Dawkins' go at 'the
God of the Old Testament' is more than
just a poke in the eye of a superhuman
being; it is a dig in the ribs of believers.
Clearly, he sees himself as striking a blow for
free speech; for he believes he is speaking
against the grain of society, a society that has
an 'overweening respect for religion':

> A widespread assumption, which nearly
> everybody in our society accepts—the
> non-religious included—is that religious

faith is especially vulnerable to offence and should be protected by an abnormally thick wall of respect, in a different class from the respect that any human being should pay to another (ibid.: 20).

Where there is an abnormally thick wall, it takes an uncommonly massive battering ram to knock it down; hence the overweening *dis*respect that he shows to religion. As it happens, I do not share his assessment of society's attitude towards religious faith. But, setting this aside, there is something to be said for the view that knocking down walls is the job of free speech. Substitute 'idols' for 'walls' and this goes to the heart of the Jewish case for outspokenness, which I outline in the third part of the essay. It can even be argued that speech is not free except where it exacts a cost. 'What is freedom of expression?' asks Salman Rushdie, whose experience with the reaction to his novel *The Satanic Verses* (1988) lends a

certain authority to the answer he gives:
'Without the freedom to offend, it ceases to
exist' (*Imaginary Homelands* [1992], quoted
in Petley 2007: 1).

Rushdie's question raises a host of others. What makes speech free—free beyond
the merely formal condition of not being
censored or banned? How free is speech
that is encumbered by 'cargo' that clutters
or obstructs the mind? In what *sense* is it
free? There is, moreover, a variety of ways
of causing offence when opening one's
mouth. Do they all exact enough cost, or a
cost of the right kind, to count? Is the bawl-
ing child in the restaurant exercising 'freedom of expression'? Is it materially
different whether the bawler is eight or 68,
sitting in a high chair or seated at high
table? Curious as these questions are, I shall
put them to one side.

By Rushdie's criterion, it is not clear
what we should say about the passage in

which Dawkins defames 'the God of the Old Testament'. It might be *intended* as a dig in the ribs of believers, but actually it is so rib-ticklingly funny that it is more likely to raise a laugh than cause an outcry. The very idea of indicting the Supreme Moral Being for almost every sin under the sun; the relish with which the charge list is unfurled; the profusion of phrases and the accumulation of commas: all of this adds up to a kind of verbal romp. Perhaps in another era it would have taken courage to publish such a sentence. Perhaps it would have shocked or discomforted a religious public. But today?

Today, a *Jewish* public might be discomforted by this passage. But while this has everything to do with being Jewish, it has little to do with being religious. It arises from the displacement of the negative attributes of God onto the Jews, a feature of anti-semitic discourse down the centuries: 'God' as a trope for 'the Jew'. The principle at work in this logic of bigotry is 'like attracts like': if 'the God of the Old Testament' is unjust, unforgiving, vindictive and pestilential, and if this God is drawn to the Jews and vice versa, it follows that the Jews themselves are unjust, unforgiving, etc. Long after God drops out of the picture, these attributes stick to the name 'Jew' like burrs; and this gets under the skin. Hence, even as I chortle at the passage in Dawkins, a little shiver goes down my spine. I feel a similar shudder every time Israel's military actions are yoked to 'the Old Testament God of wrath and carnage', to quote from one website.

This is not to suggest for one moment that there ought to be a gag order on cynics who cast aspersions on the good name of God. They are in good company. One rabbi whom I know wrote in his synagogue newsletter that he has 'a lot of difficulties with the way God is described in much of

the Torah and liturgy'. He sees it as something with which to wrestle. He is not the
only one. There is a long tradition in Judaism of wrestling with God. It goes back to
Jacob, whose prize for staying in the ring all
night was the grant of a new name: 'Israel',
literally 'he who strives with God' (Genesis
32:29). When you grapple with an omni-
potent adversary, you cannot afford to give
any quarter. So, from one Jewish point of
view, there are no holds barred: cynics do
your worst.

Yet viewed from another angle, the
question takes on a different aspect and
there is something to be said for a mod-
icum of sensitivity, if not self-restraint. For
when scorn is poured on 'the God of the
Old Testament' it can easily overflow its
banks. Without anyone intending it or
knowing it, a free-thinking attack on an
idea—the idea of the divine in Judaism—
degrades into an antisemitic discourse

about 'the Jew'. You don't have to be Jewish to find antisemitism offensive. As with any other form of bigotry, it is an affront to our common humanity. Being Jewish, of course, might enable you to recognize antisemitism when others do not—or lead you to imagine it's there when it isn't, a point to which I shall return in Part Three.

But what is Judaism? We are not yet done with this question that, at the outset, I said comes first. Not that there is a hope in heaven of putting it to rest. (Dream on, God.) What we find will be finding enough, even if it is rough and raw, if it helps us get the Jewish case today in focus. It will do if it conveys the *flavour* of Jewishness.

Calling Judaism Judaism

Let's pick up the enquiry from the point where I expressed a qualm about the word 'Judaism' on account of its suffix: the 'ism' ending that could suggest a system of belief or set of principles. It could but need not. And if we go back to the Greek word, *Ioudaismos*, which the English word translates and from which it ultimately derives, we see that it doesn't—or didn't.

The antiquity of this word is significant for our enquiry. It is older than Christianity, going back to a time that pre-dates 'the framework problem'. It can be found in the second book of Maccabees—which is in neither the Jewish nor Protestant canon—a book written in Greek at least 100 years before Jesus was born. The book tells the stirring story of how Judah Maccabee and his brothers, 'the brave champions of Judaism', led a revolt against Antiochus IV, ruler of the Seleucid Empire, who sacked Jerusalem in 167BC, massacred the inhabitants and set out to consolidate his rule by a process of systematic Hellenization. The Maccabeans recovered the Temple, liberated Jerusalem and 're-established the laws by then all but abolished' (*The New Jerusalem Bible* 2:21–2). This is, of course, a telling of the story of Chanukah, of Hebrew (good) versus Hellene (bad).

It might clarify matters if we slightly misspell the English translation of *Ioudais-mos* and say as follows: The Maccabeans were 'the brave champions' of *Judah-ism* (or *Judea-ism*): they were heroes of the people of Judea, the biblical 'land of Judah': *national* heroes fighting for the Judean way of life. This casts a new light on that troubling suffix. Parallels are perilous but, roughly speaking, the 'ism' in 'Judaism'—more precisely, the *'ismos'* in *Ioudaismos*—functioned like the 'ism' in 'Hellenism'—the *'ismos'* in *hellenismos*: it indicated a civilization.

Fast forward a couple of thousand years or so and the *Judeans* have morphed into the *Jews*. Wherever the Jews go, they carry their culture—their Judaism—on their backs; or, rather, in their books: their book

of books—their bible. They have not so
much scattered as proliferated into different kinds and denominations; so that in a
sense there is no longer Judaism in the sin-
gular, but many Judaisms: variations on an
ancient Hebrew theme. The theme is the
thing—if anything is: it is the story that is
told by the text they carry with them. Every
time they open the pages of the book or
unroll the scroll, there they find themselves.
That is to say, they encounter a people, *am
yisroel*, the people of Israel dwelling in the
text—*literally* the people of the book—and
they bond. Their word is their bond. 'Their
scripture is our script,' they say, 'their narrative our narrative.'

If this recalls Ruth the Moabite saying
to Naomi the Israelite, 'Your people shall
be my people,' it should; for Ruth, as I read
the Book of Ruth, is a model for what it is
for an individual to *lay claim* to Jewish
identity. She is like the Children of Israel at

Sinai—choosing her luck—except that she's one and not many. It is no accident that her great-grandson is the great King David. But I digress, doubly, and also anticipate the argument at the end of this essay.

To resume: opening the book together, finding their place in the text, is a collective reading that writes the entire congregation of readers into the sinews of the Hebrew scripture, chapter and verse, thereby *themselves* becoming 'the people of the book'. It is an *active* reading, always refiguring the work. In 'Our Homeland, the Text', George Steiner suggests 'the definition of a Jew as one who always has a pencil or pen in hand when he reads'; in other words, one for whom reading is a form of writing, which is to say a *development* of the text. He writes:

> The community can be defined as a concentric tradition of reading. The Gemara, the commentary on the Mishna, the collection of oral laws and prescriptions

which make up the Talmud, the Midrash, which is part of the commentary pertaining particularly to the interpretation of the scriptural canon, express and activate the continuum of Jewish being (1997: 307–8).

Readings of readings, words about words, along with their translation into deeds: this developing tradition, in a manner of speaking, is Judaism; or as close as we get to the thing itself, a thing that is never settled for it is always in the making. What to make of it: that is the question for anyone who lays claim to it.

The Cultures of the Jews

Is it a religion? Paradoxically, the category 'religious' had no purchase in the world of the ancient Israelites and the nations around them with their many gods. You do not call something X except to mark a difference from Y. Where there's no Y, there's

no X. Where there was no 'secular', there
was no 'religious'. Nonetheless, hovering
over the entire text, like a spirit over the
deep, is a celestial character who, whether
in a petty, bloodthirsty, misogynistic, homo-
phobic, racist, infanticidal, genocidal, filici-
dal, pestilential, megalomaniacal,
sadomasochistic, capriciously malevolent
frenzy, or in a rare moment of benevolence,
or from sheer boredom, creates heaven and
earth. And true, the people that appear in a
starring role in the narrative become 'a king-
dom of priests' by entering into a covenant
with this same character. And, certainly,
today we would call this narrative 'religious'.

But it is a religious *narrative*; and stories
can be taken in various ways, with pinches
of salt, grades of literalness, shades of irony.
In the passage I have quoted from Steiner,
he fastens on the core rabbinic commen-
taries and the community of readers that
forms around them. But numberless Jews
have wandered from this particular commu-

nity; and, as the rest of his essay makes clear, the text that is the Jewish 'homeland'—the Hebrew scripture—is also home to traditions of reading that we would not call 'religious'. It is a textual territory inhabited by readers with various habits of mind and living diverse lives; yet all of them somehow *Jewish*.

It comes to this. What *was* Judaism? The civilization of the Judean people. What *is* Judaism? The cultures of the Jews, whether we parse those cultures as 'secular' or 'religious'. It is less a religion and more a mosaic. Naturally, there are fellow Jews who will disagree; who limit 'legitimate' Judaism so as to exclude the so-called secular forms—and most varieties other than their own. But the shoulders of the Hebrew scripture are broader than the shoulders of the people who carry it with them wherever they go; broad enough to support them all or at least to sustain the arguments that divide them—and thereby unite them.

Besides, if Judaism were purely and simply a religion, then 'secular rabbis' would not be ordained in seminaries in Israel and the US; but they are. And 'a secular Jew' would be a contradiction in terms; which it isn't.

The *breadth* of Judaism and, as it were, its length, extending back in time to an era when the terms of reference of the word were so different, give Jewish identity a certain texture. Instead of the smooth, mutually exclusive surfaces of 'the religious' and 'the secular', you get a rough-hewn fabric with threads woven through it that sometimes overlap, at other times diverge. Among other things, this makes for a complex sensibility. At times it makes for touchiness. Without a feel for the *texture* of Jewish identity, this touchiness can be quite baffling.

Frankly, it can be baffling anyway. I sometimes wonder whether *taking* offence isn't as much part of a Jewish way of life as *giving* it. I am reminded of the story about

Moishe and the racist comedian. Moishe
went with Mary, his Catholic friend, to a club
one evening, where the non-Jewish enter-
tainer told one racist joke after another. It
was unrelenting. Blacks, Hispanics, Asians,
Kurds, Arabs, Muslims, Catholics: just about
every ethnic and religious group on the
planet were the butt of his humour except
Jews. 'You got off lightly,' said Mary, when
the show was over. 'What do you mean?'
asked Moishe indignantly. 'I was deeply
offended. Once again we see how the world
is against us.' 'Against *you*?' asked Mary
incredulously. 'But there wasn't a single antisemitic joke.' 'Exactly!' exclaimed Moishe
meaningfully. 'Always we are excluded.'

It sometimes seems that an entire
people—mine, I suppose—are perpetually
broyges: Yiddish vernacular for offended,
angry, embroiled in an argument that never
seems to end. Perhaps that's what happens
in time to an eternal people.

ENLIGHTENMENT PIETY

At this point, I seem to hear an objection. It goes something like this:

> It's all very well to make pedantic distinctions about the meanings of words and to crack ethnic jokes, but this is neither a purely academic subject nor a frivolous one. You've made your point that some Jews are secular (which is not exactly a revelation); perhaps now you can focus on those who are not. For there is a larger context. The resurgence of faith in the twenty-first century poses a threat to the modern world, giving rise to a battle for the Enlightenment. Enlightenment values are under attack. Reason itself is at risk. If we give in to the demands of believers, speech will be censored. We won't be free to speak our minds, nor read the books or watch the plays and films we choose. As for the classroom, we'll end up teaching our children myths about creation instead of scientific facts.

> In the Jewish case, it's Judaism the *reli-gion* that's the main issue: it's as plain as the nose on your face. (No offence intended.) So, get serious and get real.

Though anonymous, my interlocutor is not entirely imaginary. Much of this speech is cobbled together, or adapted from, remarks that can be found in the public domain, especially in circles that can loosely be described as 'progressive'. Many people today believe that a liberal attitude to free speech goes hand-in-hand with being secular-minded and scientifically-minded; and vice versa. The notion that we face a 'battle for the Enlightenment', a battle being fought on several different fronts, is a commonplace. Thus, my interlocutor speaks for many people. In formulating this objection, I am seeking to put thoughts into words, the better to answer them.

And I do have an answer; roughly, it consists of the rest of this essay. This is not

to say that I reject outright what the interlocutor says. For, up to a point, the objection speaks for me too. I have no wish to
live in a society where people are not free to
speak their minds; where the giving of offence is automatically an offence in law;
where we treat one another like spoilt children, walking on tiptoe for fear of treading
on each other's delicate digits; where we are
subject to the tyranny of the sensitive. I welcome not only the mark the Enlightenment
has made on our civil and political arrange-
ments in modern liberal democracies but
also the deep traces it has left on other
human traditions, not least Judaism, which,
from its Near Eastern beginnings to the
present day, for better and for worse, always
has taken the impression of the times and
places in which it has found itself. It has
certainly inflected my own take on Judaism
(see 'The Jewish Case Today'). The thought
of creationism in the science curriculum

appals me. And I admire some of the per-
sonalities of the Enlightenment precisely
for the battles, intellectual and political,
that they fought in their era. Had I been
around at the time, as likely as not, I like to
think, I would have been of their number.

But equally I am tired of Enlightenment piety. I do not mean the shibboleths
of the eighteenth-century *philosophes*. I am
referring to the uncritical adulation, even
idealization—even idolization—of their
movement that I detect in the voice of my
interlocutor. Actually, what I have in mind
is not so much the hero worship of ances-
tors—such as Voltaire, 'Father of the Enlightenment', of whom more in a
moment—a tiresome trait that is common to
many cults and not peculiar to this one, but
its misapplication to our own predicaments.

In particular, the point of view that
engenders my interlocutor's objection is a
major obstacle to understanding, and

engaging with, the Jewish case. The Enlightenment is also a topic *for* this case, a suit-
able subject for treatment, as we shall see. I
shall, therefore, tackle this objection at
some length, after which I shall resume the
main argument of the essay from the point
where I have left it.

Rubbing Shoulders with Voltaire

There are several reasons why I am scepti-
cal of the way the Enlightenment is wheeled
in to the contemporary debate. For one
thing, it is lazy thinking. It is easier to bring
a readymade vocabulary to the table, relying
on thinking done in an earlier age, than to
try to confront present-day issues on their
own terms. This is not to say that lessons
cannot be learned from the past, or that
there are no lines of thought that extend
across periods of time. But the learning and
the extending, if they are to be done intelli-
gently, cannot be done mechanically—as

though the underlying issues were un-changing and it is only their dress, as it were, that changes from one epoch to another.

Moreover, adapting the metaphor, there is such a thing as hiding behind the skirts of the Enlightenment. The point I am making here is the opposite of the point that is frequently made against people who object to a cartoon or a play that satirizes them or lampoons their convictions. Such people, it is said, are hiding from the glare of public scrutiny; and the charge some-times sticks. In other words, when people take offence, it can be a way of fending off legitimate criticism and self-criticism. But this cuts both ways. *Giving* offence is no more self-validating than *taking* offence.

Let's say Dick—it could be any Tom, Dick or Harry—draws a cartoon of Moses in the shape of a bomb falling on Gaza. He might be making a general point about religion being the cause of all wars; or a

specific point about the way the *halachah*
(Jewish religious law) has been used to justify the actions of the Israel Defence Forces
(IDF); or giving an atheist's view of 'the
God of the Old Testament'. In other words,
his purpose might be satirical. But it could
be something else: Dick might be a bigot or
bully, someone who gets a kick out of rubbing up a minority group the wrong way.
Suppose this is the case. And suppose he
succeeds: the Chief Rabbi and the Board of
Deputies of British Jews condemn the publication of the cartoon in the London
Guardian. Dick writes an indignant blog
protesting, 'The Enlightenment is under
threat.' This is what I mean by hiding behind its skirts: pretending to others or to
yourself that you are a hero when in fact
you are a heel.

'Even so,' says my interlocutor, 'Dick
should have the right to publish his cartoon. As Voltaire said, "I disapprove of what

you say, but I will defend to the death your right to say it." That's what Enlightenment defence of liberty was all about.'

I'm glad my interlocutor said that. It misconstrues Voltaire's remark so spectacularly that it gives me an opportunity to make the point about Enlightenment piety more clearly than I might otherwise have done. As it happens, Voltaire's remark was not Voltaire's: the utterance never passed his lips (Knowles 2006: 55). But let that go: I'm willing to grant that it is the sort of thing he *might* have said. The problem is that the aphorism has taken on a life of its own and has lost its moorings altogether. It floats in the cultural ether without any ballast, so that anyone might pluck it out of the air and attach it to whatever they feel like saying. In fact, there was a specific context for the remark that was (not) made by Voltaire; and the context is crucial.

The case concerns the French philoso-
pher Claude-Adrien Helvétius who, in
1758, published *De l'esprit* (On the Mind),
in which he argued for a deterministic view
of human nature. Voltaire, who had taken a
paternal interest in the younger man, was
not exactly impressed with the thesis or the
work. Moreover, as S. G. Tallentyre explains
in *The Friends of Voltaire*, he was offended by
the fact that, 'much worse than all',
Helvétius 'has actually compared *me*—ME—
to two such feeble, second-rate luminaries
as Crébillon and Fontenelle!' (2004: 196).[2]
But his protégé was a fellow *philosophe*.
Thus, Helvétius and Voltaire were broadly
in the same intellectual and cultural camp.
This is the first point to note.

The second is that *De l'esprit* quickly became notorious and 'was furiously attacked
in the religious papers'. Church and State
linked arms against the book. The Arch-
bishop of Paris declared that it 'struck at
the roots of Christianity'. It was condemned

by the French parliament and, on 10 February 1759 'publicly burned by the hangman'. Tallentyre comments:

> What the book could never have done for itself, or for its author, persecution did for them both. 'On the Mind' became not the success of a season, but one of the most famous books of the century. The men who had hated it, and had not particularly loved Helvétius, flocked round him now (ibid.: 198).

Who were these men who had hated the book and not particularly loved its author? They were not 'the enemy'. They included Turgot, Condorcet and Rousseau. They were, so to speak, members of the Enlightenment party. Rallying round Helvétius, they were coming to the aid of a beleaguered comrade. Tallentyre continues:

> Voltaire forgave him all injuries, intentional or unintentional. 'What a fuss about an omelette!' he had exclaimed when he heard of the burning. How

> admirably unjust to persecute a man for
> such an airy trifle as that! 'I disapprove
> of what you say, but I will defend to the
> death your right to say it,' was his atti-
> tude (ibid.: 198–9).

There's the phrase. The words, as Tallentyre emphasized later, were hers, not his
(Kinne 1943: 534). She was trying to cap-
ture Voltaire's attitude to the affair. Thus it
is that in the first decade of the twentieth
century (her book was published in 1907)
she coined the remark widely regarded as a
byword of the Enlightenment. It was, I em-
phasize, Voltaire's attitude to the Helvétius
affair that the remark was intended to cap-
ture. It got its sense from the context and
the context was this: a band of rebels bond-
ing against the combined power of State
and Church.

This is the point my interlocutor spectacularly misses: the weightiness of the issue,
the specific gravity of the circumstances.
Dick's imaginary baiting of a minority group

does not quite equate with standing up to the might of the French establishment in the middle of the eighteenth century. To suggest otherwise is faintly absurd and trivializes the attitude struck by Voltaire and the ringing line misattributed to him. Despite the dismissive quip about an 'omelette', I do not think Voltaire would have defended to the death Helvétius' right to say boo to a goose or, for that matter, to pick his nose in public, however offensive that would be to some people and as much as Voltaire himself might have disapproved. For the cost of such things is piffling.

This is not to say that Dick should be prevented from publishing his measly Moses cartoon, although his right in this matter, such as it is, does not impose a duty on a publisher to publish it. It is only to say that it is neither necessary nor appropriate to bring in the whole panoply of the Enlightenment in order to make the point.

Moreover, the disposition of the *philosophes* towards censorship is neither altogether clear nor straightforward. The Enlightenment historian Peter Gay remarks: 'Obsessed by enemies, not all of whom were imaginary, they were likely to treat criticism as libel and jokes as blasphemy. They were touchy in the extreme' (1966: 16). This might call to mind certain 'touchy' minority groups today, not all of whose enemies are imaginary. D'Alembert, co-editor of the *Encyclopédie*, one of the defining works of the French Enlightenment, 'petitioned the censors to stifle his critics' (ibid.). Even Voltaire, judging by what he writes about the Greeks and the execution of Socrates, seems to have thought that permissiveness could go too far. Accusing Aristophanes of having 'prepared the poison' with his send-up of Socrates in *The Clouds*, he writes:

> An entire people, whose bad govern-
> ment authorized such infamous liberties,

well deserved what happened to it: to become slaves of the Romans and today of
the Turks (1972: 50).

What is Voltaire implying? That the
government of Athens was wrong to 'autho-
rize' the performance of this satirical play?
That it should have censored certain
scenes? I'm not sure. But I cannot imagine
him 'defending to the death' Aristophanes'
right to caricature Socrates. He would have
been more likely to challenge him to a duel.

In any event, Dick is no Helvétius. But
when he puts himself forward as a cham-
pion of the Enlightenment, and when my
interlocutor defends him by invoking
Voltaire, then the act of publishing the
Moses cartoon becomes a noble piece of
derring-do. This is heroism by association.
At a stroke, Dick finds himself in the company of the good. Rubbing shoulders with
Voltaire, the latter's virtue rubs off on him.
An image of himself flashes across Dick's

mind: a wry face with a sardonic grin, crowned by a wig of flowing locks, and a witty apophthegm on his lips. He cuts a fine figure in his mind's eye, does Dick. Dick: Are you reading me? (Reader: Does the wig fit?) Then kindly note: offence intended.

The Enlightenment as a Contemporary Myth

'Since you imagine him to be a bigot or a bully,' interposes my interlocutor, 'forget Dick. Suppose it is Tom or Harry who draws the Moses cartoon intending, in good faith, to make a political point about the use of the Torah to justify the bombing by Israel of Gaza. Doesn't this make a difference?' Certainly, it makes *a* difference. It removes the element of hypocrisy or self-deception. However, the problem with my interlocutor's initial speech—the problem that underlies 'Enlightenment piety'—goes deeper than this difference. It is twofold:

the Enlightenment as a contemporary myth and Judaism as an Enlightenment myth.

By 'myth' I do not mean fiction as opposed to fact, as when we say that it is a myth that Voltaire spoke the phrase 'I disapprove of what you say . . .' In the sense in which I am using the word, Voltaire himself, though a figure who belongs to history, is also a constituent of a myth. Like Jason and the Argonauts, Voltaire and the other *philosophes* are part of the cast of characters in a *foundational story*: a story that is constitutive of a whole way of looking at things. In this case, the story defines and entrenches modernity, or a certain idea of what modernity consists of. This is what I mean in speaking of the Enlightenment as *myth*.

In the story I have in mind, the forces of Reason and Unreason do battle with each other, a battle fought on at least three fronts: freedom versus censorship, secularity versus religion,[3] science versus myth. So, this is a myth that is incapable of recognizing itself *as* myth; for if it did it would contradict its own storyline. Such, more or less, is the foundational story embedded in the initial speech made by my interlocutor. From this perspective, a case like Tom's or Harry's is the latest episode in an epic duel that spans the ages.

To an extent, as we learn from Gay, this is the Enlightenment's own myth of itself:

> The *philosophes* liked to visualize themselves re-enacting historic battles, to denounce religious fanaticism and popularize Newton wrapped in the toga of Cicero or Lucretius. This is how they gave their polemics the dignity of an age-old struggle between reason and unreason, a struggle that had been fought and lost in the ancient world and was now being fought again, this time with good prospect of success (1966: 32).

However, the fit of myth to reality in the eighteenth century was better than in the

twenty-first. Take the issue of freedom versus censorship. Naturally, the *philosophes*
tended to align this issue with the opposi-
tion between the secular and the religious;
or, more precisely, the secular and the cleri-
cal. The hands of the Church were all over
the body of the State: power was wielded
with a devout fist. The *philosophes* had no
record, memory or experience of secular
regimes. They were innocents. We, with
Hitler's Nazi Germany, Stalin's Soviet
Union, Mussolini's Italy, Mao Zedong's
China, Pol Pot's Cambodia and so on in our
past, are not. We know better. We know that
gloom can come from light; that the bliss of
dawn can turn to darkness at noon. Time
has spawned tyrants of a different stripe
from the ones the *philosophes* knew, tyrants
that many of them would have thought in-
conceivable.

And yet, the seeds of such tyranny were
also sown at the time. While confirming
that 'the French Enlightenment' was indeed

'the herald and source of modern liberal governments', the Introduction to *The Blackwell Companion to the Enlightenment* nevertheless continues thus:

> On the other side, there arose in 1793–4 a new absolutism, supposedly of the people but really of leaders speaking in their name, who presumed to have the keys to a happy, just, orderly society; men who attempted to impose the control and conformity of a totalitarian society. The roots of that kind of thinking, too, had been implanted by Enlightenment writers (Crocker 1995: 9).

The allusion, of course is to the Reign of Terror in the French Revolution. Barely four years after the 1789 Declaration of the Rights of Man and Citizen, this regime, with its notorious guillotine, became the cutting edge of enlightenment.

Thus, the conjunction between two of the signature struggles of the Enlightenment—freedom versus censorship and the secular versus the religious—was coming apart at the seams from the outset. With the passage of time, they become what they are today: two separate issues that sometimes overlap, not two fronts—or sides—in the same conflict. It is useful to recall that the free expression publication *Index on Censorship* was first published in 1972 as a response to the show trials of dissidents by the secular Kremlin, not by the Vatican.

The difference made by time is even more profound on another front: the fight the *philosophes* waged against myth (belief, faith, superstition) in the name of science. This is not a fight that can simply be carried forward from their era to ours, if only because the very meaning of the terms over which they fought has been altered in the heat of intellectual battle. Suppose a mineral ore of indeterminate composition were inserted into a fiery furnace. And suppose that eventually two or more metals were separated out—and also transmuted into different substances. This, roughly, is the process that the categories of science, myth and the rest have undergone. Or, to vary the metaphor, we can say, in the *light* of the arguments of the past, we are in a position to see these categories differently.

In their light we can see this; which is as much as to say that *for us*, in *our* time, *this* is what *enlightenment* means. And sure, it is a battle: a struggle to see clearly when so much dust is raised on all sides. Often it is the same dust kicked up by both sides. Certain believers known as Creationists muddy the logical waters by treating the first chapter of Genesis as though it were a contribution to natural science. Certain non-believers do likewise when they call the idea of God a 'hypothesis' or when they say: 'So the most basic claims of religion are scientific. Religion is a scientific theory' (Dawkins 1994). On their (joint) account, the following two

statements are on the same logical plane
and consequently in conflict with each
other: (a) 'In the beginning God created
the heaven and the earth'; (b) 'In the beginning there was a big bang'. For us, enlightenment comes with the dawning of the
thought that (a) and (b) might not be made
of the same mettle.

This thought is not likely to dawn on
my interlocutor. It does not fit the schema
of the larger story in which several different
controversies are collapsed into a single
'battle for the Enlightenment'. This
schema—the structure of the myth that the
Enlightenment has become—is a nest of
ideas within ideas. It is a mare's nest; and
in this section, for fear of being ensnared,
I have barely tangled with it. Suffice to say
that, in order to have a liberal attitude
towards freedom of expression, it is not
necessary to dismiss religion as either hocus-
pocus or the fount of all evil. Nor, if your

purpose is to *influence* the religious, is it an intelligent thing to do; it is hardly enlightened self-interest.

Moreover, like the moon, the Enlightenment has its dark side. Which brings us back to Judaism.

Judaism as an Enlightenment Myth

On one subject at least, the clear-sighted Voltaire had a blind spot. Walter Laqueur observes that he 'had nothing but contempt for the Jews' (2006: 71). This is borne out by what Voltaire wrote in his *Philosophical Dictionary* (1972): 'It is with regret that I discuss the Jews: this nation is, in many respects, the most detestable ever to have sullied the earth' (quoted in Sutcliffe 2003: 233). The fact that this remark appears in his entry on 'Tolerance' is rather droll. There again, if tolerance means putting up with the existence of a group you detest the most, then it could not be more apt.

Voltaire, says Adam Sutcliffe in *Judaism and Enlightenment* (2003), saw the Jews as 'the intolerable that must nonetheless be tolerated'. They were nonetheless intolerable.

In and of itself, this is not an indictment of the Enlightenment. One blind spot does not a dark side make, nor is it uncommon for heroes to have flaws. But Voltaire's contempt for the Jews was more than merely idiosyncratic: it was ideological. 'For Voltaire, Judaism signifies primitivism, legalism, and blind reverence for tradition: the obverse of his own Enlightenment values of progress and rational enquiry' (ibid.: 232). More to the point, many of his fellow *philosophes* saw Judaism in exactly the same light: as the negative to their positive. Sutcliffe again:

> In much Enlightenment thought, the vital conceptual space of that which is most deeply antithetical to reason— Enlightenment's defining 'Other'—was occupied above all by the Jew. Rational

inquiry opposed Jewish legalism; belief in progress opposed Jewish traditionalism; the scholarly, urbane, cosmopolitan citizen of the Republic of Letters opposed the petty-minded, mumbling ghetto rabbi (ibid.: 5).

'Much' is not 'all': Sutcliffe is careful not to exaggerate the point. There were 'shifts and ambiguities of Enlightenment thought concerning Judaism', as well as differences from one country to another. Moreover, one of the leading figures of the German Enlightenment was Moses Mendelssohn, an observant Jew, widely seen as 'the father of the Haskalah' (the Jewish version of the Enlightenment), whose impact on modern Judaism is far-reaching. Also on the credit side, liberal political reforms inspired by Enlightenment thought contributed significantly to the legal emancipation of Jewry in many European states. On the other hand, 'much' is not 'nothing':

the fact remains that many Enlightenment
thinkers saw Judaism as their principal foil.

True, it was not their primary target:
Christianity was their chief *bête noire*. But
when the *philosophes* looked behind the New
Testament, what did they see? They saw the
Old, the Hebrew scripture, the bible of the
Jews, the root, as it were, of the evil. Indeed, Sutcliffe says, 'for many radicals nothing was more satisfyingly disruptive than
the mockery of this text.' As Ecclesiastes
might say if he were alive today: 'There is
nothing new under the sun.' At the same
time, the 'otherness' of Judaism, along with
its popular caricature, was part of the
'cargo' of the general culture of Europe,
something handed down from generation
to generation; a gift, in a way, of Christianity to the Enlightenment. Thus, for Judaism
it was a double whammy, a case of 'the
enemy of my enemy is my enemy too.'

Furthermore, as if two enemies were
not enough, the *philosophes* looked to
Greece for their inspiration, thus reviving
the spectre of that very Hellenistic culture
against which the ancient Judeans, led by
Judah Maccabee and his brothers, had
fought. This is reflected in the subtitle, *The
Rise of Modern Paganism*, of Volume 1 of
Gay's classic study, *The Enlightenment*
(1966). It was also expressed in the approach that the *philosophes* took to history,
making the ancient Greeks, rather than the
biblical Jews, into 'the fathers of true civilization'. Gay explains:

> Their exaltation of Greece contradicted,
> boldly and deliberately, the traditional
> Christian view of history; it shifted atten-
> tion away from one people to another—
> *from the Jews to the Greeks*—and elevated
> critical thinking into the distinctive mark
> of historical periods (ibid.: 72, emphasis
> added).

When Gay calls the opening section of his opening chapter 'Hebrews and Hellenes' he is signalling that, in the Enlightenment rewriting of history, the difference between the two peoples is fundamental. For it is not just a matter of two *peoples*, nor is it purely a theory about the past. 'Hebrew' and 'Hellene' (following the usage introduced by Heinrich Heine) pick out the parties to a timeless conflict, a 'conflict between two irreconcilable patterns of life, thought and feeling':

> As the Enlightenment saw it, the world was, and always had been divided between ascetic, superstitious enemies of the flesh, and men who affirmed life, the body, knowledge and generosity; between mythmakers and realists, priests and philosophers (ibid.: 33).

In this Manichean understanding of humankind, 'Hebrew' denotes the party of the first part (superstitious mythmakers and priests), 'Hellene' the party of the second (body-affirming realists and philosophers). Hellene good, Hebrew bad. And if the *philosophes* saw themselves as the Hellenes of their day, they saw the Jews—along with the Christians—as the Hebrews. In short, in what seems to have been the dominant view, Judaism was not just another religion; it was an integral, negative element in the Enlightenment's founding myth.

If Arthur Hertzberg is right, this dark side of the Enlightenment cast a still darker, more sinister, shadow over the Jews of Europe. In *The French Enlightenment and the Jews: The Origins of Modern Anti-Semitism*, he argues that '[m]odern, secular anti-Semitism was fashioned not as a reaction to the Enlightenment and the Revolution, but within the Enlightenment and Revolution themselves' (1970: 7). He adds: 'Some of the greatest of the founders of the liberal era modernized and secularized anti-Semitism too' (ibid.). Laqueur concurs:

> Seen in historical perspective, the ideas
> of the Enlightenment led to the emanci-
> pation of the Jews, but they also
> contributed to the emergence of modern
> antisemitism, particularly in France
> (2006: 72).

Possibly so; but they also contributed to the
rejection of modern antisemitism. The
record is mixed; and, while Hertzberg's
thesis gives an extra twist to the knife, my
argument does not need it.

My interlocutor began by scolding me
that 'this is neither a purely academic subject nor a frivolous one.' Quite; and the fact
that the Enlightenment held Judaism
largely in disdain is neither a trivial point
nor a purely academic one, especially in the
context of a discussion of the Jewish case. It
ought to give pause. A reader might even
feel, given the context, that my interlocutor's objection is in bad taste. However, I
am not relying on this sensibility. Rather, I
have been arguing against the whole point

of view to which the objection gives expression. Oddly, it is a view that was at home in the late and unlamented Bush era—not because of its content but on account of its reductive dualism. Like 'the war on terror' and 'the clash of civilizations', 'the battle for the Enlightenment' divides humanity down the middle. In this case, the forces of good are secular progressives while the religious are the axis of evil: the dividing line is different but the principle—polarization—is the same. And it leads to the same botched understanding. In a complex world, a world of dappled things, only a case-by-case approach is enlightening. As the eighteenth-century cleric Bishop Butler is alleged to have said: 'Every thing is what it is, and not another thing.' Nothing could be plainer—unless it's the nose on my face.

Which brings me back to the point where I left off, just before I was interrupted by my interlocutor with the quaintly modernist voice.

THE JEWISH CASE TODAY

In a way, Bishop Butler's truism is falsified
by the Jewish case. Yes, in a given epoch it
is what it is. But in time—the millennia it
has taken for the ancient Judeans to turn
into the present-day Jews—it becomes another thing: not altogether different but not
at all the same. In this third and final part
of the essay, I choose to focus on the case
that presents itself today. To what extent it
fits a pattern from the past I shall refrain
from saying; for this is not what interests
me most. I choose to focus on the present
partly because this is the emphasis in
Judaism—a thoroughly *this*-worldly tradition—and because what interests me most is
the here and now. It interests me because it
concerns me. So, I do not broach my subject as a disinterested party.

I see this essay as an intervention in a
public debate in which, in any case, I am a
participant. I am not sure that I would be
writing this if it were otherwise. I am part of

the case that I am discussing—part of the problem, if you will—and I speak to it from the inside.

Today, the Jewish *case* is dominated by the Jewish *state*. I use the popular sobriquet for the State of Israel, which, for all sorts of reasons, is problematic. Nonetheless, it is precisely insofar as Israel is seen this way, by Jews themselves and by others, that it looms so large in the landscape of Jewish sensibilities. Not *all* roads in this terrain lead to Jerusalem; but enough do enough of the time to warrant putting Israel at the centre of this discussion. Besides, there is an urgency to this matter that makes it more than topical. For the sake of what is at stake, it is imperative that we discuss, openly and lucidly, the state of the discourse about Israel.

Many Jewish people are made uncomfortable by aspects of this discourse. However, discomfort, in and of itself, is no argument. It is certainly not decisive. In

setting the limits of acceptable discourse, it
is the *grounds* for discomfort, not discomfort
as such, that count. King Ahab or Ahab the
King (the king) undoubtedly felt discomforted by the strictures of Elijah, whom he
called 'you troubler of Israel' (1 Kings 18:
17). And, despite the prophet's riposte, 'It
is not I who has brought trouble on Israel,
but you,' Ahab was right; and not only
about Elijah. As a breed, the Hebrew
prophets were intent on making trouble;
trouble was their trade. They gave offence
to ruler and to people alike, discomforting
them to the core.

I am sharply critical of the limits set in
mainstream Jewish circles to the expression
of opinion about Israel. But, bearing in
mind the persistent 'othering' of Judaism, I
prefer to develop a critique from within—
confronting Judaism with itself—rather
than judging these limits from outside.
Confrontation with itself seems to me to lie

at the heart of the tradition. As I have asserted elsewhere, 'To take self-criticism out of Judaism would be like taking the light out of a candle or the heat out of a flame: it would mean taking the "Jewish" out of the Jewish people' (Klug 2004: 382). Keeping the figure of the discomforting prophet before my mind's eye, and drawing on three staple ingredients of Judaism—rejection of idolatry, respect for human dignity and commitment to argument—I shall outline a Jewish case for outspokenness.

So, there is the 'Jewish case', the subject under discussion, and a 'Jewish case', the argument that I shall be making about it. And just as I have not set out to give a comprehensive treatment of the one, so I shall only give the rudiments of the other. In this final part of the essay, my limited aim is to introduce the issues and to lay a basis for a certain way of approaching them. This essay, a little like Judaism itself, is work in progress.

Disambiguating Zion

Israel, as 'the Jewish state', is an expression of Zionism. In recent years, Zionism has taken a religious turn. It is true that, from the outset, there was an overtly religious faction within the movement. However, the current emphasis began only after the June War of 1967, in which Israel acquired, among other territories, the West Bank, which roughly corresponds to the biblical regions of Judea (south) and Samaria (north). This signalled the rise and rise of the religious settlers' movement. But it would be a mistake to imagine that the Jewish *religion* lies at the heart of the Jewish case today. Jewish identity, as I argued earlier, has a texture that defies the distinction between 'religious' and 'secular'. This is not to say that the distinction never applies; of course it does. But even when it does, often there are complexities that the distinction cannot cover, depths of feeling and association that it is unable to reach.

In his essay 'Zion', Steiner writes:

> The relations of a Jew to his or her identity can be so opaque, so stressful and replete with historical, social and psychological ambiguities, that these define, if definition is allowed to include undecidability, the very condition of Jewishness (2008: 86).

This is the place from which to start if we want to have a handle on the sensibilities that many Jewish people bring to the debate about the Middle East. Zion by any other name—'Israel', 'Jerusalem'—is as ubiquitous in the Jewish imagination as it is ambiguous. Its multiple meanings might not be altogether separable. And yet, it is worth trying to disambiguate the concept; unless we can distinguish between its various strands, we shall not be able to understand the magic that it weaves.

Consider this headline from the 6 o'clock evening news on BBC Radio 4, 10

February 2009: 'The people of Israel are voting for a new government.' 'The people of Israel': if this seems to ring a bell then it should. I count three. The first is for that ragtag collection of tribes that congregate in the pages of the Hebrew scripture and who, offered a code of conduct at Sinai, say: 'Yes, we accept.' This is 'the people of Israel' *inside* the text. The second is for the Jews who have carried that scripture to the corners of the earth and who, every time they peer into it, say: 'Yes, that's us.' This is 'the people of Israel' *outside* the text. The third is for a diverse population—Jews, Muslims, Christians and others—that constitutes the citizenry of a country in the Middle East. This is 'the people' of 'Israel'.

The third bell rings the changes: a shift of register from text to state that I have indicated with the repositioning of the quotation marks. But this is not a shift that registers on the ear, not when your head is humming with the simultaneous peal of all three bells. Even knowing what is intended—obviously the reference in the news headline is to the Israeli electorate—the inward ear cannot help but hear the overtones of the phrase. 'The people of Israel' strikes a chord; and this harmonic contains the key to a complex sensibility.

There is an entire vocabulary like this: words and phrases associated with Zionism that reverberate in the corridors of the Jewish imagination. 'The very name of the movement,' observes Hertzberg in *The Zionist Idea: A Historical Analysis and Reader*, 'evoked the dream of an end of days, of an ultimate release from the exile and a coming to rest in the land of Jewry's heroic age' (1997: 16). In other words, it evoked the eschatological vision of the Hebrew prophets. Similar associations arise with 'the very name of the nation', as Jacqueline Rose points out in *The Question of Zion*

(2007). Imagine if Israel were not called
Israel but, say, Western Palestine or The
Theodor Herzl Republic: the resonances—
of the eternal hope of an eternal people—
would not resound. Yet, for most of its
career, Zionism has been predominantly—
even aggressively—a secular movement.
Hertzberg points out that 'modern Zionist
ideology' set out to give a 'radically new
meaning' to the old messianic concept. No
doubt; but the language has a life of its
own. Never mind the ideology, feel the
poetry.

The poetry is in the prose. The music
of Zionism is fusion: sounds from tradi-
tional liturgy melded together with the jar-
gon of a secular political terminology. The
'goal of our revolution,' said David Ben-
Gurion in 1944, '. . . *is the complete ingather-
ing of the exiles into a socialist Jewish state*'
(Hertzberg 1997: 618). It is a perfect example of the genre; you could almost hear

'revelation' for 'revolution'. Four years later, the Proclamation establishing the State of Israel, teeming with biblical allusions without ever quite mentioning God, writes Ben-Gurion's script (sans the socialism) into the state's certificate of birth. The effect is to solemnize: to elevate the status of the new Jewish state into something higher than a civil institution but a little lower than the angels. Thus, in ordinary Zionist parlance, Jewish immigrants to Israel do not merely acquire citizenship: they 'make *aliyah*', the Hebrew word for 'ascent', a term packed with religious significance, carrying the implication of being summoned or called; as though becoming an Israeli were entering a higher state.

But it is not just the language of politics; it is the language per se that is packed with more meaning than its words can contain. Until it was revamped or reinvented in the late-nineteenth century in the context

of the project of 'national revival' (or re-
visal), Hebrew was primarily a sacred
tongue. In a letter to Franz Rosenzweig,
dated 26 December 1926, Gershom Scholem
asks: 'What will be the result of updating
the Hebrew language? Here is part of his
answer:

> Is not the holy language, which we have
> planted among our children, an abyss
> that must open up? People here do not
> know the meaning of what they have
> done. They think that they have turned
> Hebrew into a secular language and that
> they have removed its apocalyptic sting,
> but it is not so. The secularization of the
> language is merely empty words, a
> rhetorical turn of phrase. In reality it is
> impossible to empty the words which are
> filled to bursting with meaning, save at
> the expense of the language itself
> (Scholem 1997: 27).

I take this to mean not that the older
layers of meaning *supplant* the newer but

that they *suffuse* them. The old words are
time capsules. They are semantic bombs.
'All those words which were not created ar-
bitrarily and out of nothing, but were taken
from the good old lexicon, are filled to the
brim with explosive meaning' (ibid.: 28);
meaning that they explode the categories
that separate the holy and the profane. As a
result, the ancient sacred tongue is no
longer purely sacred and its modern secular
version is not simply secular, a linguistic
state of affairs that is explored in depth in
the technical work of Ghil'ad Zuckermann
and others (see Yadin and Zuckermann, in
press).

There are, of course, regions of Modern
Hebrew where the words are not taken from
'the good old lexicon'. This, it might seem,
weakens Scholem's argument. However, in
the first place, no region of a language is an
island. In the second place, the old system
of pronouncing *Classical* Hebrew with which

Ashkenazi Jews such as I grew up, has been largely replaced by the *Modern*. This means that 'the sacred tongue', used in the sanctuary of the synagogue, now *sounds* like the language spoken in a Tel Aviv shop or on an Egged bus. The similarity of sound tends to blur two lines of demarcation: one between the secular and the religious, the other between the groups that I distinguished earlier: 'the people of Israel' (Israelites and Jews) and 'the people' of 'Israel' (Israelis).

Where the ear hears little difference, it is harder for either the heart or the mind to make distinctions. This does not mean that the different identities are obliterated. But they are leaky: they bleed into each other: they blend or fuse. They become, in Steiner's word, 'undecidable'.

And underneath it all: the bedrock of historical experience, the persistent 'othering' of Judaism in Europe and the concomitant persecution of the Jews. The persistence—into modern times—is the crucial factor. Expulsions from England and elsewhere in the Middle Ages is one thing, but pogroms in Russia in the late-nineteenth century another. The Dreyfus Affair in France, the rise of antisemitic parties in Germany and Austria, the growth of anti-Jewish legislation in Eastern Europe, the ascendancy of the Nazis and the implementation of 'the Final Solution', which did not distinguish between religious and secular Jew: all of this has engendered a widespread distrust of 'the world' and a sense of betrayal after the bright promise of the Enlightenment. Along with this goes a deeply ambiguous ambition for a place to be Jewish: a Jewish place; a place that is both *apart from* and a *part of* 'the world'; a miraculous place.

This is the place of Israel—not on the planet but on the plane of imagination—for

many Jewish people. But even when it is
not, Israel is rarely politics as usual. On the
subject of offence, both giving and taking, it
is impossible to understand the Jewish case
today without appreciating the eminence of
Zion. Zion stands out like a city on a hill (if
it is permissible to compare a thing to itself). It is too massive to miss, too ethereal
to pin down. Bursting with meaning, it fills
the air with nuances, as thick as dandelion
seeds, whenever the State of Israel is the
subject of argument. (Self-censorship, almost, prevents me from saying: the lion of
Judah is a dandy lion.)

Consequently, with Israel as the subject,
feelings among Jewish people often seem to
run higher than the level of the argument
itself.

Arguing Over Israel

The best way to catch nuances is via in-
stances, three of which I shall discuss, two

in this section and one in the next, where I
introduce the case for speaking out. In the
compass of this essay, it is not possible to do
justice to the issues raised by these examples. I shall try to bring out some of their
complexity and, at the same time, to illus-
trate the complex sensibility that Jews generally—me included—bring to the issues.
Since I am speaking to the subject 'from the
inside' I shall speak my mind. But, in this
section, my main aim is to bring different
facets of each controversy to light and to
show how and why argument over Israel is
about more than Israel the State. For Israel
is more than the State.

The three examples that I have chosen
all arose in the context of Operation Cast
Lead, Israel's three-week military offensive
in Gaza in December 2008 and January
2009. Although they overlap, each has features that make it distinctive. Each has
been, and continues to be, a touchy subject.

The first concerns an image involving
the Israeli flag in which either the Nazi
swastika replaces the Star of David or the
flag and swastika are linked by an equals
sign. This image was used, though not for
the first time, by demonstrators in various
cities protesting Israel's actions in Gaza. I
have seen the image described by a Jewish
observer this way: 'the Jewish Star of David
equated with the swastika'. This description
is a tad misleading. It is true that the six-
pointed star on Israel's national flag is,
twice over, a Jewish symbol. First, it is—or
has become since the nineteenth century—
a symbol used by individual Jews and Jewish institutions, such as synagogues, to
signify their Jewishness. Second, Jews in
Nazi-occupied Europe and in concentration
camps were made to wear the symbol as a
badge, setting them apart as Jews. It is per-
fectly understandable that a Jewish observer,
conscious of these associations, would view

the matter under the description I have quoted: 'the Jewish Star of David equated with the swastika'. And what could be more offensive than to equate the victim with the perpetrator?

But is this the equation that the protestors themselves are making? Not on the face of it. Ostensibly, the equation is with the flag of a state—Israel—and not with a symbol of Judaism. The state chooses to identify itself with a Jewish symbol, which makes it difficult for critics to cite the national flag without seeming to refer to Jews in general. Looked at this way, any offensiveness would seem to be wholly in the eye of the beholder.

Yet, if Judaism or Jewry is not the intended target, why choose a swastika? In view of the Jewish genocide perpetrated by the Nazis, is not the choice of a Nazi symbol pointed: pointing to the Jewish character of the state?

But is it? After all, the epithet 'fascist' or 'Nazi' is a familiar form of hyperbole— almost de rigueur in some political circles— for denouncing opponents. Nor is this confined to the sphere of politics. Adolescents call their parents 'Nazis', their parents call traffic wardens 'Nazis', and traffic wardens probably think that the stingy councils that pay them a pittance are Nazis too. Moreover, Israel is not the only example of a state whose flag is equated with the swastika. As I write, I have in front of me a photo of a peace rally in the United States where the marchers are carrying a banner that shows the US flag connected to a swastika via an equals sign. I am sure there are other examples. What is the difference in the case of Israel? Why, I ask myself, am I sickened by placards that twist the Star of David into a crooked swastika? What is it about this image that is so chilling?

Because it seems like more than mere hyperbole. Because it feels that more than a symbol is being bent out of shape: that the Jewish experience at the hands of Nazi Germany is being mocked or diminished or traduced. Because by and large Israel is seen, by Jews and non-Jews alike, as 'the Jewish state', and so the message that the image seems to be sending is this: the Jewish state is to the Palestinians what the Nazi state was to the Jews. But the Nazis were murderous *because* they were Nazis: it was written into their creed. From which it seems to follow that the Israelis are murderous *because* they are Jews: it is written into *their* creed. In other words, murderousness is as much the essence of Judaism as it was the essence of Nazism.

Not many people would endorse this conclusion if it were spelled out (although I can think of at least one person who would, citing 'the Old Testament God of wrath and

carnage' as irrefutable proof). And I am not
suggesting that this conclusion is in the
minds of protestors who make the equation.
Nor am I suggesting that it follows by the
inexorable laws of logic. But it is there, if
only as a noxious connotation, curled up
like a worm inside the image. Or so I per-
ceive. I do not say that fellow Jews all share
my perception and revulsion. It is a complex matter. But many, regardless of their
politics, will feel, like me, repelled.

I was not on marches where placards
with this image were displayed. And
marchers are a motley crew. Like the mixed
multitude that Moses frogmarched out of
Egypt, they are not all savoury characters.
But nor are they all seething with hate.
Some of the protestors who stepped out
under the aegis of this image are, I am sure,
decent human beings whose views about
Israel's actions in Gaza are not very different from my own. I might even agree com-

pletely with what they say. But if they asked me to join them under their banner I would have to reply, adapting a phrase that wasn't Voltaire's: I approve of what you say, but I wouldn't be seen dead in your company.

The horrendous events in Gaza moved one celebrated British playwright to put pen to paper. Caryl Churchill's 10-minute drama *Seven Jewish Children: A Play for Gaza* (2009), written in the midst of hostilities, has stirred up a controversy that is set to run much longer than the play's own brief run at the Royal Court Theatre in London in February 2009. This is the second of the three examples that I shall discuss.

The play comprises seven scenes, each of which takes place at a different point in time. Without being specified, it is clear that each scene corresponds to a particular period or landmark event in modern Jewish and Israeli history, beginning, it seems, with the Nazi Holocaust, or possibly an ear-

lier period of persecution, such as the
pogroms in Russia in the late-nineteenth
century, and ending in the present with
Gaza. In each scene, a number of speakers
discuss the question of what to say to a
young girl: seven Jewish children, one per
scene, for seven different periods.

The children are present through their
absence; they haunt the play from the
wings. (In this sense they are like the
Palestinians.) All the dramatis personae are
Jewish adults, 'the parents and if you like
other relations of the children' (ibid.: 1).

It is what the adults say, or contemplate
saying, to their children, (together with
what they do not say) that has provoked
some prominent Jewish figures to accuse
Churchill of antisemitism. Several call the
play a 'blood libel', reviving hoary legends
of Jews killing non-Jewish children. One
writer sees 'a stage populated by monsters
who kill babies by design' and who 'admit

to feeling happy when they see Palestinian "children covered in blood"'. Another describes it as a modern 'mystery play', a form of mediaeval theatre 'which portrayed the Jews as the demonic killers of Christ'. Several commentators pick out the line 'tell her we're chosen people', which comes near the end in a relatively long and unlovely speech; a speech which, when I saw the play, did indeed make me squirm in my seat.

But discomfort, in and of itself, is no argument. The play, without question, is edgy. And certain lines activated the same alarm bells in my head as the alarm bells that went off in the heads of the critics from whom I have quoted. It is not as if the rivers of antisemitism have run dry; they continue to flow underground, welling up to the surface from time to time as muck. And yet, I reject the suggestion that this play is one of those cesspools.

How come? Same play, same lines, same shards of language that cut deeply into the flesh of Jewish people, but I reach the opposite conclusion. Why?

Because Operation Cast Lead is not an antisemitic fantasy projected onto Jews but a reality inflicted on Gazans. Because Israel did actually launch a brutal campaign that really did kill hundreds of children and babies. Because there are different characters in Churchill's play, voices that contradict each other from the word go, and there is nothing to suggest that the ultra-Zionist character at the end, the one that speaks the long and unlovely speech, is meant to represent all Israelis, let alone the Jewish people. So this is not remotely a mediaeval 'mystery play' where the Jew equals 'the Jews'. Even this character never 'admits to feeling happy' when seeing Palestinian children 'covered in blood'; she or he only admits to this: 'tell her all I feel is happy it's

not her.' Which reminds me of an e-mail I
received from an actual pro-Israel group
three days into the ground phase of the
campaign, which said that IDF soldiers
were fighting 'in order to protect Israeli
children', adding, 'unfortunately, this did
not come without losses.' For an instant I
had the illusion of compassion. But the e-
mail continued: 'We mourn the loss of five
IDF soldiers, since the beginning of the
ground operation. May their memory be
blessed.' As if the hundreds of Palestinians,
perhaps one-third of them children, killed
by the IDF did not count, were not worth a
mention, let alone a blessing for their
memory. The character at the end of the
play is disturbing. But 'a stage populated by
monsters who kill babies by design'? Do me
a favour! This is sheer fantasy, a fantasy
projected onto Churchill; antisemitism, as it
were, in reverse.

'But are there not other voices inside
Israel, let alone within the wider Jewish
world? If Churchill had wanted to avoid
stigmatizing Jews in general, would she not
have given as much space, with as much
force, to a Jewish voice that opposed Israel's
actions or, at least, grieved for the Palestinian losses?'[4] First, there *are* other voices in
the play. Second, you must remember the
play's *raison d'être*. It is subtitled *A Play for
Gaza*; it was written when Israel's one-sided
onslaught was at its height. Her purpose at
the end, clearly, was to foreground and
highlight the kind of voice that has, unfortunately, to this point prevailed, even though
it does not have the last word. The play is a
lament for Gaza; but look at it also as a
warning—blunt, humane and probably
valid—about the trajectory that Zionism has
taken.

In the debate over Israel, there is a
familiar pattern in which the antagonists

appear to be locked in an embrace, a little
like love. Critics, crossing an invisible line
in the sand, find themselves accused of anti-
Jewish hatred—or *self* hatred if Jewish.
They react by accusing their accusers, alleg-
ing that so-called antisemitism is nothing
more than a machination of 'the Israel
lobby'. At once, this is seized upon as an
antisemitic slur; which in turn is denounced
as a Zionist smear. Round and round they
go, down and down they go, in a circle that
gets ever more vicious.

In a letter to the London *Independent*
responding to her critics (one in particular),
Churchill enters this circle. The accusations
against her, she suggests, are intended 'to
distract attention from Israel'. I think this
misses the point; it certainly misses a point
that I have been making in this section. For
reasons that I have tried to elucidate, Israel
is a lightening rod for many Jewish people.
You can feel the electricity whenever you go

near the subject. I do not say that the accusation of antisemitism is never a cynical ploy. But mostly it is an authentic visceral reaction when someone appears to have crossed that line in the sand. I am not *defending* this; apart from anything else, the cry 'antisemitic' is heard so often nowadays that it has come to sound rather like 'wolf'. But if an authentic cry, howsoever mistaken, is dismissed as fake, this merely gives the vicious circle of offence another spin.

Likewise with branding a playwright anti-Jewish because she is pro-Palestinian. 'But despite what you say, surely this play really *is* antisemitic. For it is so one-sided.' So was Israel's ruthless onslaught on Gaza. Saying this I run the risk—more likely a cast iron certainty—of being called self-hating. Which brings me to the third example that I wish to discuss and the final stage of the argument of this essay.

Laying Claim to Judaism

On 11 January 2009, a rally in support of
Israel, organized jointly by the Board of
Deputies of British Jews and the Jewish
Leadership Council, was held in London's
Trafalgar Square.[5] A number of us, under
the auspices of Independent Jewish Voices
(IJV), gathered on the fringe of the square
for a counter rally. To get to our site outside
Canada House we had to run a gauntlet of
jeers. 'Traitors', 'cowards', 'scum' and other
epithets were hurled in our direction. When
the rally was over, some of us were spat at
and called '*kapos*' (a derisory term for certain Jewish inmates of Nazi concentration
camps who were seen as collaborators). The
contempt and hatred for us, as Jews, was
palpable. But it did not come from fanatical
jihadists or fascists in the British National
Party. Nor even from a Caryl Churchill play.
It came from fellow Jews. A ritual was being
enacted in which we were being symboli-
cally 'othered'.

In a way, I am glad of it. Being othered reminds me that I am a Jew, especially when I consider what provoked this behaviour: the expression of open dissent about the State of Israel. For what does this mean? What does it mean when you are expected to stand solidly with a state? When you must declare that you love it before you may question it? When criticism must always be balanced with praise? When all the fears and hopes of a people are placed in its hands? When to distance yourself from it is to invite contempt, and to approach it is to ascend, as if it were resting on a pedestal? What does this mean? It amounts to this: Israel is not a normal, ordinary state in the minds and hearts of many Jews. It means the state has been made into a statue. You can call it a cause or ideal. But it is an idol by any other name.

Which is no idle thing. In fact, nothing is weightier in the Hebrew scripture than the matter of idolatry. What, in heaven's name, does it mean to be Jewish if not to knock statues off their pedestals? If, whatever our political opinions, we cannot rise above the State of Israel and put it in its place, if we do not reduce its status to that of a mere thing among things, then we are not Jews, or we are Jews in name only. But *things* can be criticized, challenged, opposed, rejected, replaced: there is not a line that you may not cross when approaching a *thing*—not in the iconoclastic Judaism to which I lay claim.

But fellow human beings are another matter. They are fellow members of the largest Jewish family in the world: the *human* family, sharing the same *bubbe* and *zeyda*, grandma Eve and grandpa Adam, through whom, in the Genesis story, they inherit the image of God. From which the Talmud derives the principle of *kevod habriyos*, literally 'honour of the created', in idiomatic English 'human dignity'. 'The

dignity of every person is sacred,' writes
Rabbi Chaim Shmulevitz, who for 15 years
was *Rosh* (head) of the famous Mirrer
Yeshiva in Jerusalem.[6] The concept, he says,
has 'overriding importance':

> Rabbinic enactments and various scrip-
> tural prohibitions are set aside when they
> conflict with human respect and dignity
> ... The concept of [human dignity] does
> not, however, stop at refraining from in-
> sulting or degrading one's fellow human
> being. One is also obligated to enhance
> and magnify the prestige and honor of
> one's fellow (1989: 242).

So, you cross any line in order to speak
out about the degradation of others: this is
a rule in the Judaism to which I lay claim.
You do not infringe this rule to support a
state, whatever your attachment to that
state. If there is anything that Jews should
always support it is justice, not a state;
especially not a state that sports the name
'Israel', not if 'Israel' stands for the top-

pling of idols (or their moral equivalent) and the pursuit of justice. 'Justice, justice shall you pursue' (Deuteronomy 16:20): this is the directive that Moses gives the people of Israel in the wilderness, the direction that he points out. And, starting with the Hebrew prophets, there is a long straggling line of Judeans and Jews, of ancient Israelites and modern Israelis, of rabbis and writers and activists, who have followed suit. Some call themselves secular, others religious, others just plain Jewish.

Between them, these two principles, the one positive (respect for human dignity), the other negative (rejection of idolatry), lay the substantive basis for a Jewish case for outspokenness. On the one hand, they motivate, on the other hand they limit, free expression of opinion about anything whatsoever. To which we can add a third—essentially procedural—principle: commitment to argument.

'Argument for the sake of heaven': this
is how the Mishna (the core of the Talmud,
compiled around the end of the second
century AD) puts it when argument is con-
ducted not for its own sake or for the sake
of winning but with a view to a higher purpose, such as truth, justice or peace. Even
God enters the argument when, for example, Abraham engages him in moral reason-
ing over the fate of Sodom (Genesis 18).
And not even God can settle the argument,
according to a remarkable tale in the Talmud. Once, goes the story, there was a dis-
pute between two rabbis, Rabbi Eliezer and
Rabbi Joshua, when a heavenly voice inter-
vened to say that Rabbi Eliezer was right.
To which Rabbi Joshua retorted, in effect,
that God has no standing. 'For the Torah
has already been given from Mount Sinai
and we pay no attention to a heavenly
voice.' God 'smiled in that hour' and said,
'My children have defeated me. My children

have defeated me' (*Bava Metzia* 59b). After quoting this passage, Rabbi Joseph Soloveitchik comments: '[I]t is as if the Creator of the World Himself abides by man's decisions and instruction' (2005: 80). Earth looks to heaven for guidance but heaven, in this story, looks back to earth. '*You* decide. Argue it out': argument for the sake of the world. (Argument for the sake if the world is argument for the sake of heaven: this, in a way, sums up Judaism for me.)

In the argument over Israel, there are no 'no go' areas except as determined by the first two principles, applied via the third. Anything goes, even discussion of the most sensitive issues, even its existence as 'the Jewish state'. And if this causes offence, tough: no political entity, no state, no object—nothing is above and beyond the reach of argument in the interests of peace, justice and truth. These are the commitments that I recognize as staple in the Judaism to which I lay claim.

Looking across the square on 11 January from our little stronghold—our little Zion—outside Canada House, we could see some of the younger demonstrators on the official rally wrapping themselves in the national flag of the State of Israel. *This*, to *me*, is offensive. For the basic design of the flag—two blue stripes against a white background—represents the *tallis*, the robe or shawl worn at synagogue services. Wearing the flag as if it were the *tallis* signifies devotion, folding Judaism into the state, making the state sacrosanct. This is nationalism. It is not anything that I can call 'Judaism'.

'But,' says a new interlocutor, quietly stepping forward from the shadows, patiently waiting for this moment, knowing from the beginning that it would come, 'if, as you have argued, Judaism is a "mosaic", if it is a set of "variations on an ancient Hebrew theme", if the Hebrew scripture is "broad enough to support them all", then who are you to rule anything out?' But it cannot support the insupportable. 'Then what is Judaism?'

That, in the end, is the question.

Notes

1 I owe this idea to Clive Lawton in private conversation.

2 It is unclear from the context whether this is intended by Tallentyre as an actual quote or an imaginative attribution.

3 The Enlightenment, for the most part, was deist rather than atheist (Voltaire being a case in point). But deism was God without religion. At any rate, it was God without *revealed, organized* religion: God as a postulate of reason, not an article of faith. Moreover, having kick-started the world, God was largely seen as surplus to requirement. It is a small step from 'not being at all needed' to

'not being at all': from deism to atheism.

4 I owe this point to Micah Smith in private conversation.

5 Part of this section is adapted from my 'A Crisis in Judaism', *Guardian*, 'comment is free' website (15 January 2009).

6 I owe knowledge of this volume to my former schoolmate James Rosenfelder, who died as I was finishing this essay.

Bibliography

CHISICK, Harvey. 2005. *Historical Dictionary of the Enlightenment*. Lanham, MD: Scarecrow Press.

CHURCHILL, Caryl. 2009. *Seven Jewish Children: A Play for Gaza*, London: Nick Hern Books.

CROCKER, Lester G. 1995. 'Introduction', in John W. Yolton, Pat Rogers, Roy Porter and Barbara Stafford (eds), *The Blackwell Companion to the Enlightenment*. Oxford: Blackwell, p. 9.

DAWKINS, Richard. 1994. 'Lecture from "The Nullifidian" (Dec 94)'. Available at: www.richarddawkins.net/article,89, Lecture-from-The-Nullifidian-Dec-94, Richard-Dawkins

———. 2006. *The God Delusion*. London: Bantam Press.

GAY, Peter. 1966. *The Enlightenment: The Rise of Modern Paganism, Volume 1* New York: W. W. Norton & Company.

HERTZBERG, Arthur. 1970. *The French Enlightenment and the Jews: The Origins of Modern Anti-Semitism*. New York: Schocken Books.

———. 1997. *The Zionist Idea: A Historical Analysis and Reader*. Philadelphia: The Jewish Publication Society.

JACOBS, Louis. 1995. *The Jewish Religion: A Companion*. Oxford: Oxford University Press.

KINNE, Burdette. 1943. 'Voltaire Never Said It!' *Modern Language Notes*, 58(7) (November): 534.

KLUG, Brian. 2004. 'A Time to Speak Out: Rethinking Jewish Identity and Solidarity with Israel', in Adam Shatz (ed.), *Prophets Outcast: A Century of Dissident Jewish Writing about Zionism and Israel*. New York: Nation Books, pp. 377–94.

——. 2006. 'The Danish Cartoons and the Voice of Reason'. *Emel*, 18: 47.

KNOWLES, Elizabeth. 2006. *What They Didn't Say: A Book of Misquotations*. Oxford: Oxford University Press.

LAQUEUR, Walter. 2006. *The Changing Face of Antisemitism*. Oxford: Oxford University Press.

PETLEY, Julian. 2007. *Censoring the Word*. London and New York: Seagull Books.

ROSE, Jacqueline. 2007. *The Question of Zion*. Princeton: Princeton University Press.

ROTH, Philip 2000. *The Human Stain*. New York: Houghton Mifflin.

SCHOLEM, Gershom. 1997. 'Thoughts About Our Language (1926)', in *On the Possibility of Jewish Mysticism in Our Time and Other Essays* (Avraham Shapira ed.,

Jonathan Chipman trans.). Philadelphia: The Jewish Publication Society, pp. 27–9.

SHMULEVITZ, Chaim. 1989. *Reb Chaim's Discourses*. New York: Mesorah Publications.

SOLOMON, Norman. 1998. *Historical Dictionary of Judaism*. Lanham, MD: The Scarecrow Press.

SOLOVEITCHIK, Joseph. 2005. *Halakhic Man*. Jerusalem: Sefer ve Sefel Publishing.

STEINER, George. 1997. 'Our Homeland, the Text', in George Steiner, *No Passion Spent: Essays 1978–1996*. London: Faber and Faber, pp. 304–27.

———. 2008. 'Zion', in *My Unwritten Books*. London: Phoenix, pp. 91–122.

SUTCLIFFE, Adam. 2003. *Judaism and the Enlightenment*. Cambridge: Cambridge University Press.

TALLENTYRE, S. G. 2004. *The Friends of Voltaire*. Honolulu: University Press of the Pacific.

VOLTAIRE. 1972 [1764]. *Philosophical Dictionary*. London: Penguin Books.

YADIN, Azzan and Ghil'ad Zuckermann. In press. '*Blorit*: Pagains' Mohawk os Sabras' Forelock? Ideological Secularization of Hebrew Terms in Socialist Zionist Israeli', in Tope Omoniyi (ed.), *Sociology of Language and Religion: Change, Conflict and Accommodation*. London: Palgrave Macmillan.